A Woven Voices and Jermyn Street Theatre
co-production

The Anarchist

By Karina Wiedman

T0347682

Winner of The Woven Voices Prize
Performed at Jermyn Street Theatre, London,
6 July – 30 July 2022

The Anarchist

Written by Karina Wiedman

CAST

DASHA	Scarlett Brookes
KATYA	Elisabeth Snegir
JOE	Ojan Genc

PRODUCTION TEAM

Director	Ebenezer Bamgboye
Set & Costume Designer	Caitlin Mawhinney
Lighting Designer	Catja Hamilton
Sound Designer	Tony Gayle
Movement Director	Adi Gortler
Movement Director	Sacha Plaige
Production Manager	Lucy Mewis-McKerrow
Stage Manager	Heather Smith
Production Technician	Edward Callow
Graphic Designer	Ciaran Walsh
Production Photographer	Steve Gregson
PR	David Burns

Cast

SCARLETT BROOKES | DASHA

Theatre includes: *Statements After an Arrest Under the Immorality Act* (Orange Tree Theatre); *Tryst* (Chiswick Playhouse); *Blood Wedding* (Young Vic); *The Taming of the Shrew* (Sherman Theatre); *Meek*, *Junkyard* (Headlong); *Macbeth* (Globe Theatre); *Educating Rita* (Oldham Coliseum); *The Merchant of Venice, Othello, I Can Hear You, This is Not an Exit, The Ant and the Cicada, Revolt. She Said. Revolt Again* (Royal Shakespeare Company); *Ghost from a Perfect Place* (Arcola Theatre); *Our Big Land* (Romany Theatre Company); *To Kill a Mockingbird* (Manchester Royal Exchange); *Ignorance* (Hampstead Theatre); *Love and Information* (Royal Court Theatre).

Television includes: *Call the Midwife* (Neal Street Productions); *The Feed* (Amazon); *Kiri*, *Damned*, *Blackout* (Channel 4); *The Scandalous Lady W* (BBC); *Misfits* (E4).

Film includes: *Morning Song* (Film 4); *Bulldozer* (Try Hard Films); *Farming* (Hanway Films).

ELISABETH SNEGIR | KATYA/ENSEMBLE

Theatre includes: *Christmas Carol: The Haunted Service* (Goblin Theatre); *Dead Dog in a Suitcase, Our House, A Midsummer Night's Dream, Pericles* (Mountview Academy of Theatre Arts); *In and Out of Chekhov's Shorts* (UK tour); *Scarlett Letter* (Dumbwise Theatre Company); *Father Christmas at the Hall* (Royal Albert Hall).

OJAN GENC | JOE/ENSEMBLE

Theatre includes: *Trade* (ELMA Productions).

Television includes: *Slow Horses* (Apple TV); *Angela Black* (ITV); *Da Vinci Demons*, *EastEnders* (BBC); *Obsession: Dark Desires* (October Films); *Hollyoaks* (Lime Pictures); *A Touch of Cloth* (Zeppotron).

Film includes: *Patient 17* (Patient 17 Ltd).

Creative Team

KARINA WIEDMAN | WRITER

Karina Wiedman is a playwright based in London.

Originally from Kazakhstan, she lived in Russia and Belarus before moving to the UK.

She trained as an actor at the Guildhall School of Music and Drama and later earned an MFA in Writing for Stage and Broadcast Media from the Royal Central School of Speech and Drama.

Her first play, *The Anarchist*, is the winner of the Woven Voices Prize for migrant playwrights. Karina addresses political traumas, stigmas and social injustice through the voices of ordinary people.

EBENEZER BAMGBOYE | DIRECTOR

For Jermyn Street Theatre: *Two Horsemen*.

Theatre includes: *Boys Cry* (Riverside Studios/Omnibus Theatre); *6 Artists in Search of a Play* (Almeida Theatre).

Theatre as Assistant/Associate Director includes: *Faustus: That Damned Woman* (Lyric Hammersmith); *A Very Expensive Poison* (Old Vic); *Three Sisters* (Almeida Theatre).

Ebenezer is the Carne Deputy Director of Jermyn Street Theatre.

CAITLIN MAWHINNEY | SET & COSTUME DESIGNER

For Jermyn Street Theatre: *Shake The City, Orlando* (Assistant Designer).

Theatre includes: As Designer: *Teechers Leavers 22* (Hull Truck Theatre); *Shake The City, The Sh*T, My Voice Was Heard But It Was Ignored* (Leeds Playhouse/UK tour); *My Old Man, Is Anyone There?* (Imagine If Theatre Company); *Frisky And Mannish: Popcorn* (Lawrence Batley Theatre); *Our Gate, A Shadow of Doubt, The Body Snatcher, Connection* (Harrogate Theatre); *Anna* (Mind The Gap Theatre Company); *There's a Dead Body in My Baby's Sandpit* (Hope Street Theatre); *The Marriage of Kim K* (The Lowry/UK tour).

As Installation Designer: *The Children's Country House* (Sudbury Hall, National Trust); *Setting the Stage* (Hull Truck Theatre); *My Three Words* (IOU Theatre Company); *Meet Your Neighbour* (Maison Foo Theatre Company).

As Assistant: *The Beauty Queen of Leenane* (Lyric Hammersmith/Minerva Chichester); *Lady Chatterley's Lover* (Shaftesbury Theatre); *Bell Bottom* (Pooja Entertainment); *Ubu: A Sing-A-Long Satire* (Kneehigh Theatre Company).

Caitlin is a 2022/23 Creative Associate at Jermyn Street Theatre. She is a Resident Designer at New Diorama Broadgate and was awarded the Evening Standard x TikTok Future Theatre Fund in 2021.

CATJA HAMILTON | LIGHTING DESIGNER

For Jermyn Street Theatre: *The Marriage of Alice B. Toklas by Gertrude Stein* (Associate Lighting Designer).

Theatre includes: *Dolly, Another America, The 4th Country* (Park Theatre); *An Intervention* (Riverside Studios); *Lizard King* (Camden People's Theatre and UK tour); *Patient Light* (The Undercroft); *I Have Heard You Calling in the Night* (Union Theatre); *Hot Gay Time Machine* (Soho Theatre); *how we love* (Arcola Outside, VAULT Festival); *The Establishment Versus Sidney Harry Fox* (Above the Stag); *Take Care, TUNA* (VAULT Festival); *Venus and Adonis* (Bussey Building); *She Sells Sea Shells* (Edinburgh Fringe); *ERIS* (Bunker Theatre).

As Associate Lighting Designer: *Running with Lions* (Talawa/Lyric Hammersmith); *Romeo and Juliet* (Regent's Park Open Air Theatre); *Botticelli in the Fire* (Hampstead Theatre); *Maklena* (Camden People's Theatre and touring).

Catja is a 2022/23 Creative Associate at Jermyn Street Theatre. She is a Resident Designer at New Diorama Broadgate.

TONY GAYLE | SOUND DESIGNER

Sound design includes: *Playboy of The West Indies* (Birmingham Rep); *Legally Blonde* (Regent's Park Open Air Theatre); *The 47th* (Old Vic); *Running with Lions* (Talawa/Lyric Hammersmith); *Spring Awakening* (Almeida Theatre); *Get Up, Stand Up! The Bob Marley Musical* (Lyric Theatre, London); *A Place For We* (Talawa/Park Theatre); *The Wiz* (Hope Mill Theatre); *Blue/Orange* (Theatre Royal Bath); *And Breathe...*(Almeida Theatre); *Gin Craze!* (Royal & Derngate); *The Living Newspaper*, *Shoe Lady* (Royal Court); *Poet in da Corner* (Royal Court/UK tour); *Beautiful – The Carole King Musical* (UK tour); *Salad Days* (UK tour); *American Idiot* (UK tour); *Songs for Nobodies* (Wilton's Music Hall & West End); *Floyd Collins* (Wilton's Music Hall); *The Wild Party* (The Other Palace); *Lazarus* (King's Cross).

Recognition/Awards: 2021 Black British Theatre Awards (BBTA) Light & Sound Recognition Award – 2019 & 2021. Alfred Fagon Award Black Champion.

Other: Wise Children Trustee, Stage Sight Co-Director, Founder of The Audio Cartel.

ADI GORTLER | MOVEMENT DIRECTOR

Theatre Movement Directing: *Borders حايس ردגה* (Drayton Arms, OSO Arts Centre); *I see in color* (Haifa International Children's Theatre Festival); *Picnic on the Battlefield* (Bilhaa Theatre); *The Canaan Women* (Myco Festival); *The Political Yoga Sequence* (The Arab-Hebrew Theatre).

As placement on RCSSD MFA: Movement Directing and Teaching: *Be My Baby*, *Mr. Kolpert*, *X*, *Foxfinder*, *Three Sisters* (LAMDA); *The Belle's Stratagem* (RCSSD).

Assistant Movement Director: *Alice* (RCSSD).

Theatre Directing: *I see in color* (Haifa International Children's Theatre Festival); *As a Matter of Fact-the Post-Truth Cabaret* (Habima Theatre, Tzavta Theatre and Haifa Theatre); *The Sun Princess* (Bilhaa Theatre).

Adi is a movement director, director, and teacher based in London. Originally from Tel-Aviv, she has a B.Ed. in Theatre Directing and Teaching and is currently completing her MFA in Movement Directing and Teaching at The Royal Central School of Speech & Drama. She is interested in human experience, and how the story is told through movement.

SACHA PLAIGE | MOVEMENT DIRECTOR

Theatre includes: *La bohème* (Nevill Holt Opera); *Europeana* (Royal Shakespeare Company); *The Skating Rink* (Garsington Opera); *FEAST* (Battersea Arts Centre).

Television includes: *The Undeclared War* (Channel 4).

Half-French half-Russian, Sacha is a performer, movement director and theatre-maker. She trained at the École Jacques Lecoq and is a founding member of award-winning Clout Theatre Companyy.

She holds an MA in Movement: Directing and Teaching from the Royal Central School of Speech and Drama and divides her time teaching, movement directing and creating with her theatre company.

She is an Associate Lecturer at Wimbledon College of Arts on the BA Acting and Performance and has taught at Rose Bruford College, ALRA, Fourth Monkey and LAMDA.

HEATHER SMITH | STAGE MANAGER

For Jermyn Street Theatre: *The Marriage of Alice. B. Toklas* (ASM).

Theatre as Stage Manager on Book: *The Baker's Wife* (Playground Theatre); *Remembering Jeremy James Bond* (Park Theatre: 200); *Our House* (Sue Townsend Theatre).

Theatre as Company Stage Manager: *Aladdin* (The Eric Morecambe Centre); *Alice* (RCSSD/Leicester Curve).

Theatre as Assistant Stage Manager: *Whodunnit [Unrehearsed] 2* (Park Theatre: 200); *Imaginary* (Sue Townsend Theatre); *Cats*, *Les Misérables* (The Little Theatre).

Heather is a recent graduate from The Royal Central School of Speech and Drama.

JERMYN STREET THEATRE

a small theatre with big stories

WHO WE ARE

Jermyn Street Theatre is a unique theatre in the heart of the West End: a home to remarkable artists and plays, performed in the most intimate and welcoming of surroundings. World-class, household-name playwrights, directors and actors work here alongside people just taking their first steps in professional theatre. It is a crucible for multigenerational talent.

The programme includes outstanding new plays, rare revivals, new versions of European classics, and high-quality musicals, alongside one-off musical and literary events. We collaborate with theatres across the world, and our productions have transferred to the West End and Broadway. Recently, our pioneering online work and theatre-on-film has been enjoyed across the world.

A registered charity No. 1186940, Jermyn Street Theatre was founded in 1994 with no core funding from government or the Arts Council. Since then, the theatre has survived and thrived thanks to a mixture of earned income from box office sales and the generous support of individual patrons and trusts and foundations. In 2017, we became a producing theatre, the smallest in London's West End. Around 60% of our income comes from box office sales, and the rest in charitable support and private funding.

★★★★★
66 **Unerringly directed ... no one in this tiny theatre dared breathe.** 99
The Observer

THE NUMBERS

Nearly **50,000** audience members have come to see our shows in our first five years as a producing theatre.

Produced **40** world premiere shows.

30 new plays have been published in the UK after starting here.

In 2020, our digital content on YouTube was viewed **117,896** times.

James Sheldon and Charlotte Hamblin in Miss Julie. 2018. Photo by Keith Pattison.

★★★★★

OVER THE YEARS

1930s	During the 1930s, the basement of 16b Jermyn Street was home to the glamorous Monseigneur Restaurant and Club.
early **1990s**	The staff changing rooms were transformed into a theatre by Howard Jameson and Penny Horner (who continue to serve as Chair of the Board and Executive Director today) in the early 1990s and
1994	Jermyn Street Theatre staged its first production in August 1994.
1995	Neil Marcus became the first Artistic Director in 1995 and secured Lottery funding for the venue; producer Chris Grady also made a major contribution to the theatre's development.
late **1990s**	In 1995, HRH Princess Michael of Kent became the theatre's Patron and David Babani, subsequently the Artistic Director of the Menier Chocolate Factory, took over as Artistic Director until 2001. Later Artistic Directors included Gene David Kirk and Anthony Biggs.
2012	The theatre won the Stage Award for Fringe Theatre of the Year.
2017	Tom Littler restructured the theatre to become a full-time producing house.
2020	Our audiences and supporters helped us survive the damaging impacts of the Covid-19 lockdowns and we were able to produce a season of largely digital work, including the award-winning *15 Heroines* with Digital Theatre +.
2021	We won the Stage Award for Fringe Theatre of the Year for a second time. Artistic Director Tom Littler and Executive Director Penny Horner were recognised in The Stage 100.
2022	We won a Critics' Circle Award for *Exceptional Theatre-Making During Lockdown* and an OffWestEnd Award for our Artistic Director.

support us

> **I recently became a Patron of Jermyn Street Theatre, as I believe passionately in the work it is doing. It would be wonderful if you could contribute.**
> *Sir Michael Gambon*

We have four tiers of Friends with names inspired by *The Tempest*. Please consider joining our Friends to support a small, independent charity that needs your help.

Lifeboat Friends
(£4.16 to £12.42 a month)

Our **Lifeboat Friends** are the heart of Jermyn Street Theatre. Their support keeps us going. Rewards include priority booking to ensure they can get the best seats in the house.

The Ariel Club
(£12.43 to £41 a month)

Members of the **Ariel Club** enjoy exclusive access to the theatre and our team. As well as the priority booking and Friends Nights enjoyed by Lifeboat Friends, **Ariel Club** members also enjoy a range of other benefits.

The Miranda Club
(£42 to £249 a month)

Members of the **Miranda Club** enjoy all the benefits of the Ariel Club, and they enjoy a closer relationship with the theatre.

The Director's Circle
(From £250 a month)

The Director's Circle is an exclusive inner circle of our biggest donors. They are invited to every press night and enjoy regular informal contact with our Artistic Director and team. They are the first to hear our plans and often act as a valuable sounding board. We are proud to call them our friends.

We only have 70 seats which makes attending our theatre a magical experience but even if we sell every seat, we still need to raise more funds. **Michael Gambon** (our new Honorary Patron), **Sinéad Cusack, Richard Griffiths, David Warner, Joely Richardson, Danny Lee Wynter, Rosalie Craig, Trevor Nunn, Adjoa Andoh, David Suchet, Tuppence Middleton, Martina Laird, Gemma Whelan, Eileen Atkins, Jimmy Akingbola** and many more have starred at the theatre.

But even more importantly, hundreds of young actors and writers have started out here.

If you think you could help support our theatre, then please visit www. jermynstreettheatre.co.uk/friends/

Jermyn Street Theatre is a Registered Charity No. 1186940. 60% of our income comes from box office sales and the remaining 40% comes from charitable donations. That means we need your help.

our friends

The Ariel Club

Richard Alexander
David Barnard
Martin Bishop
Katie Bradford
Nigel Britten
Christopher Brown
Donald Campbell
James Carroll
Ted Craig
Jeanette Culver
Valerie Dias
Robyn Durie
Shomit Dutta
Maureen Elton
Anthony Gabriel
Carol Gallagher
Roger Gaynham
Paul Guinery
Diana Halfnight
Julie Harries
Andrew Hughes
Margaret Karliner
David Lanch
Keith Macdonald
Vivien Macmillan-Smith
Nicky Oliver
Kate & John Peck
Adrian Platt
A J P Powell
Oliver Prenn
Martin Sanderson
Nicholas Sansom
Andrew WG Savage
Nigel Silby
Bernard Silverman
Anthony Skyrme
Philip Somervail
Robert Swift
Paul Taylor
Gary Trimby
Kevin Tuffnell
Ian Williams
Marie Winckler
John Wise

The Miranda Club

Anthony Ashplant
Derek Baum
Geraldine Baxter
Gyles Brandreth
Anthony Cardew
Tim Cribb
Sylvia de Bertodano
Anne Dunlop
Nora Franglen
Pirjo Gardiner
Mary Godwin
Louise Greenberg
Ros Haigh
Phyllis Huvos
Frank Irish
Marta Kinally
Yvonne Koenig
Hilary Lemaire
Jane Mennie
Charles Paine
John Pearson
Iain Reid
Martin Shenfield
Carol Shephard-Blandy
Jenny Sheridan
Brian Smith
Dana-Leigh Strauss
Mark Tantam
Esme Tyers
Jatinder Verma

Director's Circle

Anonymous
Michael & Gianni Alen-
Buckley
Judith Burnley
Philip & Christine Carne
Jocelyn Abbey & Tom
Carney
Colin Clark RIP
Lynette & Robert Craig
Flora Fraser
Charles Glanville &
James Hogan
Crawford & Mary Harris
Judith Johnstone
Ros & Duncan McMillan
Leslie Macleod-Miller
James Simon
Marjorie Simonds-Gooding
Fiona Stone
Peter Soros & Electra
Toub
Melanie Vere Nicoll
Robert Westlake & Marit
Mohn

Woven Voices

Woven Voices is a London-based award-winning production company. As an international company, it seeks to weave together different voices, native and migrant, in order to champion cross-cultural work. Recent projects for stage include *Subject Mater* (Edinburgh Festival Fringe, Fringe First Award); *Bruises* (Tabard Theatre) and *Tartuffe* (Theatre Royal Haymarket). In 2020, the company launched the podcast series Migreatives, featuring interviews with migrant creatives working in the UK.

Woven Voices is led by Nadia Cavelle, Zachary Fall, and Ben Weaver-Hincks.

The
Woven Voices
Prize

The Woven Voices Prize is an open invitation to all migrant writers in the UK and Ireland to share outstanding new work for the stage, presented by Woven Voices and Jermyn Street Theatre, in partnership with Actors Touring Company, PROJEKT EUROPA, Migrants in Theatre and Phosphoros Theatre.

The aim of the prize is to celebrate and platform migrant writers, an underrepresented demographic on UK theatre stages. Around 14% of the UK population and 37% of London's population were born outside the UK. The Woven Voices Prize celebrates this rich source of creativity. It is a proclamation of a global, multicultural Britain and Ireland, and it opposes the 'Little England' mentality of isolationism.

In 2022 the judging panel featured Maria Aberg, Arifa Akbar, Ebenezer Bamgboye, Ameera Conrad, Jatinder Verma, & Timberlake Wertenbaker.

The Anarchist by Karina Wiedman was the inaugural winner of the prize in 2022. The runner-up was *Unburied* by Jimin Suh. The finalists were *The Waiting Room* by Akshay Sharan, *Coconut Republic* by Butshilo Nleya, *The Dead Box* by DHW Mildon and *Tikkun Olam* by Teunkie Van Der Sluijs.

THE ANARCHIST

Karina Wiedman

Acknowledgements

I would like to say a special thank you to Stephen Laughton, Marco Moro, Anna Patarakina and Wyn Jones for their relentless support and guidance.

My deepest gratitude to the Nick Hern Books team for publishing my first play, and to Jermyn Street Theatre along with Woven Voices for bringing it to life.

I also wish to thank Natalia, Raisa and Diana for their invaluable insight and inspiration for this story.

K.W.

4

Characters

DASHA

DAD
PETYA
MOTHER
BOSS
KATYA
LUBA
ALEX
RUSLAN
SAN SANYCH
JOE
GALINA
GRANNY
OFFICER
GYNAECOLOGIST
NURSE
POLICEMAN
DRIVER

Other characters can be recorded voices or played by the actors playing Katya and Joe.

This text went to press before the end of rehearsals and so may differ slightly from the play as performed.

DAD. Get in here.

DASHA (*to us*). I resist.

He pulls me up from underneath the table.

DAD. Stand in the corner.

DASHA (*to DAD*). No!

(*To us.*) I slap him on the chest.

He lifts me up with his left arm and with the right continues arguing with Mum.

He drags me through the kitchen door into the corridor and puts me down.

DAD. Stand still and face the wall.

DASHA. I turn.

An inch from my nose I see a giant black hole.

Eight eyes. Eight legs. Hairy.

(*To DAD.*) Spider!

DAD. Stop it.

DASHA (*to us*). He presses me from behind.

I stand here alone. Facing it.

An inch away.

Stares at me.

One-on-one. Fair.

The sound of the doorbell ringing. She looks at the time.

Half-seven.

I get up. Covered in sweat. Menopause girl.

But there are worse things I went through.

Pause.

Half-naked, in boxers and a loose tank top, I jump through the doorway.

In front of me stands Petya, our postman.

Since I was eleven, he's brought us letters and parcels.

(*To* PETYA.) Long time no see. What have you got?

PETYA. Sign here first.

DASHA. You are shaking. Been drinking?

PETYA. The elections. What if it's him again?

DASHA (*to us*). And just in front of me he turns from a wise old fox into a worn-out boozer.

I tilt my head to one side, put my hand on top of his shoulder and say...

Nothing.

We stare at each other holding the same thought of inevitability.

We both know that today Lukashenko is going to be elected again.

Petya looks at the tattoo on my thigh.

PETYA. Is it Stalin?

DASHA (*to* PETYA). Che Guevara.

Pause.

(*To us*.) I get to the kitchen, pour hot water into a cup, and add instant coffee: three in one.

In front of me is this large yellow plastic envelope. I can guess what's inside.

It's one of those things that can turn your life around... or cut it in half.

Stomach is churning, hands are wet from the nerves. I wipe them against my chest.

Fuck it.

I tear it apart.

It's from the United States embassy.

Inside: a large 'don't open' envelope, a congratulations letter and passport.

I flip through the pages and find the immigrant visa.

I'm officially a Green Card winner.

Pause.

Could it be a scam?

Am I making a mistake?

Can Mum see me now?

In moments like this I believe that the dead spy on me.

(*To her imaginary mother.*) 'Yes, I'm doing it for you.'

(*To us.*) I turn but the chair is empty.

She used to sit over there, between the table and the refrigerator.

Mama.

When she leaned back her curly black hair became magnetic and turned her into a Frankenstein.

Pause.

(*To her imaginary mother.*) So it's not a bad offer, huh? Maybe I should take my swimsuits and a pair of nineties sunglasses like in *The Matrix*... You would've gone without blinking, got yourself a little place by the ocean. And you did go... in your own way.

The sound of the alarm on her phone.

(*To us.*) I run into my room.

I unzip my sports bag, and begin stuffing it with bras, cables, headphones, make-up, jewellery, hormone pills, vitamin E... and B12.

Then the Pringles can, documents and cash.

There is no cash.

Pause.

Fine. I'll get to work, ask for the latest paycheque and then go straight to the airport.

The only way out is to leave before they announce the result.

They'll put up barricades, border restrictions and unleash the riot police.

In the morning they'll shut the streets, roll the tanks in and begin the arrests.

Everyone who tries to leave will be taken in for days, weeks, years.

If I don't board the flight tonight, I'll be here forever.

Pause.

I close the bag and sit on the bed, holding the letter in my sweaty palm. Squeezing it hard.

I take a final look at the room: wardrobe, TV set, books, empty picture frames, white sheets.

I stand up and put my hand on the wall.

Here hangs a black flag with a circle-A that I pinned in nineteen eighty-nine.

I tear it apart.

If hope dies last, then it was buried long ago.

Pause.

From the wardrobe I take my mother's dress.

She never reached her menopause, lucky girl.

And this dress... this dress still smells of her.

Pause.

I put it on.

Lighter. Click. Deep breath.

I haven't left the house without a puff since I was twelve.

I check the plugs, put on my shoes and sigh to myself: go with God.

I'm out.

I see flags and crowds of protestors. Soon we'll know the count.

The sound of the tram.

The tram is packed.

I land on someone's toes.

He doesn't mind. He's in his twenties and smells of machine oil.

His eyes look at me from time to time and he blushes.

I smile.

Maybe I remind him of his old teacher or worse, his mother.

Sweat rolls down my calves. In his ear – a familiar sound.

A rock song plays.

That song was on my first vinyl record *Rock on Bones*.

Nineteen eighty-seven. In the Soviet Union rock just became legal.

Flashback. DASHA *becomes her younger self in 1987.*

I'm thirteen and I want one thing: not to feel lonely.

Mum and I live in a one-bedroom flat. We waited in a queue for it.

We don't buy flats here; we get them for free.

Some queue their whole life and never get one.

I remember my dad was pissed off that I wasn't a boy.

Because then we would have gotten a two-bedroom.

He left when I was six... I haven't seen him since.

Pause.

I play *Rock on Bones* so loud that the neighbours can't hear me screaming.

I rub my ear with an ice cube. Then I hold a piece of apple under my earlobe and stab it with a needle.

I bleed everywhere.

It's unbearable.

I throw up.

At school the kids call me a weirdo. Teachers too.

And they might be right.

There might be something wrong with me.

The sound of the door opening.

MOTHER. Dasha, turn it off!

DASHA. It's Mum. She runs straight to the bathroom.

I follow her.

(*To* MOTHER.) How's work?

(*To us*.) I jump on the washing machine. She is in the middle. Undressing.

She looks different today. Stumbles as she gets into the bathtub then laughs to herself.

As she bends for the soap, I see scratches on her back.

(*To* MOTHER.) Where did you get those from?

MOTHER. A cat.

DASHA (*to us*). She pulls the shower curtain.

Her dress is covered in stains. I lean forward to pick it up.

MOTHER. Leave it!

DASHA. She works at a clothing store. How did a cat get in there?

Mum is covered in soap. Water pours down her smooth skin and hair.

I used to think that one day I would have her long black Jewish hair and round breasts.

One day I'll pluck my eyebrows and shave these long straight legs.

One day I'll wear a fur coat and the baker will give me bread for free.

I turn to the mirror and instead of a young version of Mum, I see a thirteen-year-old Ozzy Osbourne.

Snub nose. Long arms. Small breasts. Wide hips. Fat calves. Short.

Hair never turned black. No curls but straight and I have a lot of it.

Pubic hair, thin hair, thick hair, long hair.

On my arms, under arms, legs, knees, toes, above my lips, inside my nose.

Eight eyes. Eight legs. Hairy.

MOTHER. Turn it off!

DASHA (*to* MOTHER). Fuck off Mum!

(*To us*.) I get out of the bathroom. Run to the sofa. Stop the record.

Music is off.

I should not have said that to her.

Mum doesn't swear, smoke or drink… but does she have sex?

Pause.

I go back to the bathroom and again I pick up her dress.

I smell it… old vinegar… man's sweat.

(*To* MOTHER.) Mum, are you seeing someone?

MOTHER. You have to stop spying on me!

DASHA (*to us*). She storms out, off to the kitchen.

Sometimes I wonder if every house in the world is filled with secrets and lies.

Do other kids behind the Iron Curtain fall asleep to the sounds of broken glass and screams?

I enter the kitchen.

She is standing there with the bottle of her drops that she keeps on the top shelf.

I want her attention. Recognition. Reconciliation.

I put my arms around her waist and look at her face.

(*To* MOTHER.) Mum, this dress… it smells…

(*To us*.) She moves away.

The sound of the drops.

One, two, three, drops she had after a bad argument with Granny.

Granny says that our family is cursed and that's why men don't stay with women.

Am I cursed too?

The sound of the drops.

Eight, nine, ten drops she had when she saw a tattoo on my wrist.

The circle-A. One day I want to become an anarchist and change the world.

The sound of the drops.

Fifty drops she'll take in five years.

She'll be on the floor, unconscious, and I'll be standing there, in the corner looking at –

Present moment. The sound of the tram doors opening.

Minsk Automobile plant. MAZ. I work here.

Inside everyone is at their desks. Grey suits. Pale faces.

I drop the bag on the floor and head to the boss's room.

Knock-knock.

BOSS. Come in!

DASHA. I enter.

The boss is in the middle, watching his favourite film *The Big Short*.

He is big and short.

(*To* BOSS.) Morning. I wanted to ask if you could give me this month's pay today?

(*To us*.) He turns.

He looks distressed.

His suit is covered in rubbish and paint.

(*To* BOSS.) What happened?

BOSS. Sit down.

DASHA (*to us*). He looks down like a little boy who is about to be examined.

BOSS. Protesters, bandits, scum! These riots are sponsored by the West, you see… these European 'talking heads' want to devour our Belarus.

DASHA. He hates the West but wears Versace, drives Mercedes and sips on Macallan.

BOSS. Tonight our own workers will be joining the anti-Lukashenko protest. It will lead to a factory strike. I can't allow it, so you have to stop them.

DASHA (*to* BOSS). Me? How come?

BOSS. You're my assistant, you can find the rebels, right?

DASHA. I don't think I can.

BOSS. Go to Sanych. He can help. But if you don't fire them, you won't see this month's pay.

DASHA. Fine.

BOSS. And bring me some coffee and jam.

DASHA (*to us*). I've been working for him for thirty years and he hasn't once said 'thanks'.

Pause.

At my desk, I cannot resist unzipping my bag and looking inside.

The envelope with the Green Card sits between the bra and the Pringles can.

I can't resist.

I turn on the screen, log in and search for flights.

Tonight, there is only one that goes from Minsk to JFK via Frankfurt.

Total comes to five hundred fifty bucks.

Pause.

In my wallet I've only got twenty and seventy-five on PayPal.

What if I use the corporate card?

The Big Short is only going to find out that I'm gone tomorrow night.

At ten he'll start calling suspecting that I slept through my alarm.

But when he doesn't hear from me after five, he's going to call the police.

I'll be in Brighton Beach by then.

So I log in and pay for a one-way business trip with his Mastercard.

Done. In six hours I'll be gone.

Pause.

He wants me to fire my own colleagues.

To him I'm an incurable type. A social parasite.

My colleagues are not like me, you see, they're loyal, grateful and kind.

If you step into our office, you won't even hear a sound.

Their retired mothers live in a blackout, they can't afford the bills.

But when their sons come in, they always have freshly baked pancakes and tea.

They spend their last rouble on a candle in church, praying for them.

How their youngest daughters fail every quiz because dyslexia is a Western myth.

How their favourite eldest girls trade books for foreign cigarettes to seduce the professors and finally pass exams.

But they sit here in their Soviet uniforms and keep silent.

How they love to joke about my tattooed legs, piercings, and toned biceps.

These women would jump at each other's throats, but when there is an odd girl, they gang up against her and instantly become best friends.

Every time I enter the toilet, they begin to shout the names of their kids, because I've never had any.

And, as if by mistake, they always give me a plus-one, knowing that I'll turn up alone.

How at every New Year's party, these men get drunk and try getting into the same hole they originally came from, promising to leave their wives.

But every morning they sit and look at their watches, hoping this minute I will break.

But I know that I'm like Perseus, if I drop my shield and look at them, I'm dead.

Pause.

I'll fire them, I don't care what it takes.

In six hours I'll be on my way to the US.

I'll never see their faces again.

Pause.

BOSS. Dasha, my breakfast!

DASHA (*to* BOSS). Almost done!

(*To us.*) I run to the kitchen.

Boil the kettle, toast the bread, jam.

The lid of the jar is tight.

I open it but it slips and spills on my crotch.

Flashback. The school bell rings. DASHA *becomes her younger self in 1987.*

(*To* KATYA.) Katya, put your pants down! Fast!

(*To us*.) I'm holding my granny's strawberry jam.

In front of me, Katya, the most popular girl in my class. She's one of the anarchists.

Today all the lessons are cancelled due to girls undergoing their first pelvic exam.

KATYA. What if the vaginist finds out I'm not a virgin?

DASHA (*to* KATYA). He'll expel you from school.

KATYA. So what do I do?

DASHA. The only way to skip the exam is to be on your period.

KATYA. Mine are two weeks away.

DASHA. I'll fix you up. And if it works, you'll have to introduce me to the anarchists.

KATYA. Alright.

DASHA (*to us*). She pulls her pants down.

I put the napkins between her legs and pour my granny's strawberry jam on top.

It looks like blood.

Katya pulls her pants up, hugs me and we run upstairs.

We join the queue.

KATYA. Wait, what about you?

DASHA (*to* KATYA). I'm a… I've done mine already.

(*To us*.) I don't want to admit that I'm a virgin, late-comer, green, old hand.

Guys make fun of nuns like me but not Katya. She's far from a nun.

(*To* KATYA.) It's your turn now, good luck.

(*To us*.) In those five minutes I am praying for Granny's jam to work.

Katya gets out.

KATYA. I'm officially a virgin, so meet you in the park at seven.

DASHA (*to* KATYA). Revolution or hopelessness?

KATYA. Freedom or death! Oh, and bring some booze.

DASHA. I'll bring the best vodka in town.

(*To us*.) I run to my granny's.

Since last year alcohol has been forbidden by law. So, most guys get drunk on window cleaner mixed with cranberry juice.

But I'm lucky, cos my gran makes her own vodka, called *samogon*.

It's illegal, but she makes good money out of it. 'Enough for you to go to college', she says.

She is more practical than Mum and I can always find a few roubles in her little vase.

I turn the key and enter.

'Granny!'

Silence.

She is out. I take my shoes off and run to the kitchen.

There's a large milk can on the stove and a tube connecting it to a bucket.

Inside are caramels and toffees. A brown mess. I taste the floating candy.

Disgusting.

I don't think I will like vodka. I've never tried it before.

In the right corner there is another bucket filled with ready-made *samogon*.

In the corridor I take an empty bottle of cologne.

Granny's customers are local alcoholics. They even drink her cologne!

But she doesn't say a thing, because of her blind faith in honest communism.

I pour *samogon* into the cologne bottle as well as the empty strawberry jam jar.

The doorbell rings.

Shit.

Who's there?

LUBA (*drunk*). It's Luba… from upstairs.

DASHA (*to* LUBA). Have you got a bottle?

LUBA. Nah…

DASHA (*to us*). I take a glass and fill it up with vodka.

(*To* LUBA.) Three roubles.

LUBA. For the glass?

DASHA. But if you don't want it—

LUBA. Please. Take it.

DASHA (*to us*). Now I've got three roubles from Luba and the other two from the vase.

Enough to buy a lipstick.

I go to Alex's. He buys cool stuff abroad and resells it here.

We call him *fartsovshchik*.

He opens the door. In his twenties. Black Mohawk, denim shorts and an AC/DC T-shirt.

ALEX. You want jeans or sneakers? Eighty roubles each.

DASHA (*to* ALEX). A lipstick.

(*To us*.) He opens a box full of lipsticks, pencils, eyeshadows.

In the store you can find only a brick-like colour but at Alex's: cherry, charcoal, ivory, moonlight green…

I grab two: cherry and lavender.

(*To* ALEX.) I'll take both.

ALEX. That's seven.

DASHA. I'll give you three and a jar of vodka.

(*To us*.) He accepts.

Even *fartsovshchiks* struggle to get booze.

I get back home, leave my hair loose, paint my lips in lavender.

With the cherry one I write 'Sonic Youth' on my T-shirt.

Tonight, Mum will call the police because her daughter didn't come home.

Pause.

I get to the park but Katya's not here.

I'm trembling. Palms are sweating and the jar is slipping.

On the bench I see a group of young guys covered in cool tattoos, iron and leather.

I hold a slippery jar under my armpit.

I see a handsome guy in torn Levi's and a biker jacket.

He is a head taller and five years older than me.

(*To* RUSLAN.) Excuse me, you seen Katya?

RUSLAN. Hey.

DASHA. Katya… she is my classmate.

RUSLAN. I think I saw you before.

DASHA. I'm Dasha.

RUSLAN. Ruslan. You wanna drink?

DASHA (*to us*). I have this feeling inside my stomach. This feeling of excitement. I want to impress him.

(*To* RUSLAN.) Sure.

(*To us*.) I hand him the jar. He takes a facetted glass and adds juice.

I take the cologne bottle from my sock.

(*To* RUSLAN.) Can you add some here?

RUSLAN. Where did you get this stuff?

DASHA. I made it.

RUSLAN. It's fuckin' great.

DASHA (*to us*). His eyes are green. Shining. I think he likes me.

He hands me the bottle. I sip. It tastes bitter.

(*To* RUSLAN.) Ruslan, are you an anarchist?

RUSLAN. Sometimes… we need more juice. You wanna come?

DASHA. Sure.

(*To us*.) He takes my hand and we go. The guys turn to us. They whisper.

I get closer to him. I've never smelled a man before.

I think of Mum's dress and how it smelled of sweat. He smells different.

(*To* RUSLAN.) I like vodka.

RUSLAN. Who doesn't?

DASHA (*to us*). I realise that I'll be the most popular girl once I start selling Granny's *samogon* to the anarchists.

RUSLAN. What are you thinking?

DASHA (*to* RUSLAN). Whether they make a pill that grows boobs.

They laugh.

(*To us*.) He puts an arm around my waist. I blush. He points at a bicycle.

RUSLAN. Let's borrow the bike and get out of town.

DASHA. We jump on the bike. Inside my body, everything turns upside down.

His face: long nose, sad eyebrows, thin lips. It feels like I've known him all my life.

What if it's true? Have we met before? He said that he had seen me.

My cheeks are burning.

I hug him from behind.

For safety, but I want to be closer.

We go. The wind blows.

Inside me: bubbles, heat, a thousand bats.

I want to scream. Laugh. Sing him songs.

Love songs.

In French. I don't speak French. I make it up.

She sings.

'Je pluen la porei
In fo je moi amore…'

I place my head on his back.

I feel safe.

But what if he finds out that I'm a freak?

A giant black hole.

Eight eyes. Eight legs. Hairy.

But maybe he is one too.

He smells of leather, petrol and cigarettes.

We pass my house, where Mum and I have been living for all these thirteen years.

We pass the school. Painted green. Lights off.

Tomorrow Katya and I will skip history class to talk about Ruslan.

We pass my mum's store and then we stop in front of a little cottage.

Single-storey. High fence. 'No dog' signs.

Is that where he lives?

Will he invite me home? Will I meet his mum? What if she doesn't like me?

Will my mum like him? He looks kind. 'Too kind for a man', Granny would say.

RUSLAN. You like raspberries?

DASHA (*to* RUSLAN). A lot.

(*To us.*) He takes me in his arms and puts me on top of the fence. I jump to the other side.

In the window an old man watches *The Office Romance*.

We move from one bush to another, picking raspberries, blackberries, gooseberries.

I don't like gooseberries, but I pretend I do. I swallow them whole.

He notices.

RUSLAN. Hey, bird, with me you don't have to pretend.

DASHA. I want to bite him.

Want to have a piece of him.

As though I'd caught him in my web.

He steps closer.

Touches me. As if by accident. His skin on my skin.

Timid. Looks away. I smile.

I get on my toes and kiss him on the cheek.

His face is boiling. My heart is jumping.

We walk.

Back to the town. Hand in hand.

I want Katya to see us. I want the whole school to see us.

I'm with a real anarchist. I want his name on my wrist.

RUSLAN. Listen, I wanna show you something.

DASHA (to RUSLAN). What if I don't like it?

RUSLAN. You can leave.

DASHA (to us). He walks fast. I gallop. He whistles a familiar tune.

RUSLAN (singing). 'Ooh, it makes me wonder...'

DASHA. Vodka makes my head spin.

We enter a garage.

It stinks of oil and petrol.

There is an old motorbike in the middle.

(To RUSLAN.) Wow. Is it yours?

RUSLAN. It's my two cylinders. I just changed the tailpipe.
I thought it was burning oil. But when I checked... no smoke
was coming out... by the way, how old are you?

DASHA. Old enough to take a ride.

(*To us.*) I feel so cool to pull out such a response. He smirks
and suddenly kisses me.

I've never kissed anyone before. His saliva is on my cheeks.

Suddenly he puts his tongue in my mouth. I laugh.

RUSLAN. Wait a sec.

DASHA. He goes to the other side and lights up a candle.

On the walls there are posters of naked girls and rock bands.

Sonic Youth, The Pixies, L7.

RUSLAN. Have this.

DASHA. He hands me a cup. I don't know what's inside it, but
I down it.

(*To* RUSLAN.) Is it true that you've seen me before?

RUSLAN. I see you *now*.

DASHA (*to us*). We sit on the floor which is covered in
newspapers and cigarette butts. *Prima*. The same ones that
my dad used to smoke.

Does he still smoke?

Where is he now?

Will I ever see him again?

Ruslan takes off his jacket and gets on top of me. He puts his
hand on my breast.

I push it away.

It's on my tummy now.

He leans back.

A stranger.

Black. Giant. Hairy.

Stares at me. I pull him towards me.

He lowers his jeans and pushes inside.

It's painful. I bite myself. He moves fast.

I look up.

Gasp.

Silence.

Gets up. Confident. Been there.

Zips his trousers. Sips from the bottle.

RUSLAN. You alright?

DASHA. I see blood. Pull my pants up.

He puts his arm around me.

I cover myself with his jacket and lean on his chest.

I feel fine. Next to a cool guy just like I wanted.

Pause.

But why do I feel so lonely?

Pause.

That was the first and last time I ever saw him.

The lunch bell goes off and we are back to the present moment.

It's lunchtime.

I skip the canteen and go straight to the factory hall to see the workers.

I repeat the plan to myself: get the names, fire them, take the money and leave.

Down the fire-exit stairs, I arrive at the bottom of the dark, greasy and noisy warehouse.

I was expecting to see the workers sitting in a circle, spraying political mottos on canvas.

Instead, they are standing at the machines with their dry yellow faces covered in mazut.

The blue overalls and white helmets make them look like little Lego toys.

They are working units, not men.

They are doing hard labour for the wealthy Western neighbour, an imaginary man they've only seen on telly, maybe in *Happy Days* or *Friends*.

I walk like an Angel of Death, inhaling gas and black oil.

They turn their heads away from me.

They know why I'm here.

Pause.

At the end of the hall sits our head engineer San Sanych.

He is dipping bread into a cup of milk but as I come in he rises and shakes my hand with both hands, like Charlie Chaplin.

SAN SANYCH. Salut! Please take a seat.

DASHA. I sit on a stool and light up a cigarette.

Chaplin turns up the radio and confides in me.

SAN SANYCH. I have sixty names of traitors. They might resist but please don't panic if…

Loud chatter from the radio. It's an interview of a local politician in support of Lukashenko.

DASHA. The radio transmission runs through me like an electric current.

I'm choking on smoke that is getting stuck in my throat like a spiral.

It's Zhenya.

He used to be our Che Guevara, an anarchist known by the nickname Joe.

I heard that in the past thirty years he changed several names, wives, teeth, faded a few tattoos and gained a few kilos.

By now I've forgotten how he looks, walks, smells – but I'll never forget the way he speaks.

Flashback. DASHA *becomes her younger self in 1988.*

JOE (*to the anarchists*). For years we were sealed with no ability to move and breathe… all living things including us were paralysed. But it's nineteen eighty-eight… and this year above my head I can feel a sliding plate. I see a crack and through this crack I see light…

We, the anarchists, are not just some gang of bandits or vandals. We are both a political and spiritual community. We're punks, hippies, top students with honours and gold medals. Over there, communists sit in disguise wearing plain sweaters with red ribbons. But here we protest with every inch of our skin… we will abolish totalitarianism!

The sound of applause.

DASHA. Joe has long hair and a golden eagle tattoo on his chest.

He is our delegate. The leader of our tribe.

He is well-read, sharp, smart. His dream was to become a cosmonaut.

But when he learnt that Soviets burnt Komarov in the sky, his boyish dream died.

Instead he sharpened his tongue and developed the confidence of a hangman.

When he discusses Kropotkin and Marx, he wears glasses with a clear lens to appear older and have more weight.

But as he falls asleep on my lap, he turns into a restless Peter Pan.

Pause.

Every Friday we gather here, at Joe's *dacha*, his summer house, our base.

I tell my mum that I'm going to sleep at Granny's.

But because it's Shabbat Granny never picks up the phone and Mum never learns the truth.

Tonight I'm going to my first ever protest led by Katya.

KATYA (*to the anarchists*). Tonight's protest is dedicated to the victims of the Chernobyl disaster… it's been two years since the explosion. The government never told us the truth. I still remember standing on the balcony and looking at the sky. The clouds were coming from Ukraine, scattering radioactive particles above our heads. (*Pause.*) In seven months my mother died. I need to know why!

The sound of applause.

DASHA. She comes down from the stand but looks sad.

I wave to her.

(*To* KATYA.) Let's sniff some gas!

KATYA. Do you have a can?

DASHA. Joe brought fresh gas for the Molotovs. I poured some into a jar.

KATYA. What if your mum asks why we smell like a petrol station?

DASHA. We'll tell her we were fixing a motorbike.

(*To us.*) We run to the toilet, lock the door and sit on the floor opposite each other.

I place what's left in the jar between my knees and squeeze it hard.

(*To* KATYA.) What you wanna be when you grow up?

KATYA. A pianist. And you?

DASHA. A spy.

They bend over the jar.

(*To us.*) In a few seconds everything smears.

Katya's hair is changing colour from black to red.

I close my eyes and sniff again.

The bathroom spins and turns red.

On the floor: knives, blades and nails.

I fly above them like Bulgakov's Margarita on a broomstick, naked.

I look down and I see how these blades turn into walls and form a labyrinth.

The room grows, but the ceiling presses me down so that I go lower and lower.

I touch the blades with my feet. Lose control of the broom. Spread my legs and jump.

I drop the jar.

Pause.

Broken glass.

KATYA *laughs.*

KATYA. What a trip!

DASHA. I feel empty.

I've been trying to fill myself up with sex, booze, gas and even Mum's drops… but none of it helps.

Pause.

JOE. It's time.

We go to the kitchen to pack our bags with clothes, posters, Molotovs.

I take two bandages, one spray and two boxes of matches.

DASHA (*to* JOE). Can you teach me how to make a bomb?

JOE. You take a bottle and fill two thirds with gas, then you add sour mash. You tear a piece of cloth, stick it inside the bottle and shake it a little. Then cut a piece of iron wire and tie it around the bottleneck. Make it tight.

Pause.

DASHA (*to us*). It's past midnight.

I hold the bottle in my hand while walking through the main streets of Minsk.

I hear the grasshoppers.

On the pavement the street lights reflect our figures in a shadow.

It is a hot summer night filled with dust and city smoke.

There are not many of us, about twenty.

We turn left and arrive at the City Hall.

Pause.

Joe whispers.

JOE. Forward.

DASHA. He takes a baseball bat out of his backpack.

Through his painted eyes a black tear rolls down his cheek but there is a smile on his lips.

He probably thinks of Komarov, Solzhenitsyn and Mandelstam.

Katya thinks of her mum.

I'm thinking only how to reach any of these windows with my first Molotov.

We step forward.

JOE. For our people!

DASHA (*to us*). We burst.

We roll out the posters and hang them on the concrete walls.

We break the windows with bats and stones.

Meanwhile, Molotovs are flying above our heads like firecrackers, spattering in the air.

The sound of sirens. DASHA *holds a Molotov with both hands.*

JOE. It's your turn!

DASHA (*to* JOE). No, Joe.

JOE. Get on my shoulders!

DASHA *jumps.*

It's time.

DASHA No, I can't.

JOE. There is a reason why you are here, don't look back.

DASHA (*to us*). I light up the wick and toss it...

But I misfire.

Present moment.

SAN SANYCH. Our *Batka*... twenty-six years and not once he's done things under pressure. We always had fair elections. I know what they want... Americans! Americans want to destroy us!

DASHA (*to* SAN SANYCH). Oh, really?

(*To us.*) If only Sanych knew about my plans.

The flight takes off in four-and-a-half hours.

I checked in and cleared the desk.

It's time to write the names on the firing templates.

(*To* SAN SANYCH.) Sanych, I can't agree more but it's time to fill in the forms.

(*To us.*) Behind him, I see a worker.

GALINA. I'm sorry... but I know what you are here for.

SAN SANYCH. Galina, leave and shut the door.

GALINA. I've got five kids, four boys and a girl... my husband is a veteran of the Afghan War.

SAN SANYCH. Those veterans are worse than foreign spies. They've been stirring against the government since eighty-nine!

GALINA. We never see daylight. We work hard. Please...

She kneels.

SAN SANYCH. Get up!

DASHA. He grabs her by the arm.

I want to smack him but I can't. I must take the damn flight.

(*To* SAN SANYCH.) Let her go!

SAN SANYCH. She's been planting a bomb behind our back!

DASHA. I've got a wild card, old twat, I'll sack you too.

(*To us*.) He offers Galina a hand.

She stands up.

As I pour myself a cup of milk, Sanych grabs it and spits into it.

Flashback. It's New Year's Eve, 1990.

GRANNY. Ptui! Dasha, move it away from me.

DASHA (*to us*). Granny hates our New Year tree. She says she's allergic.

But it looks gorgeous to me.

I dressed it in lights, glitter and toys: matryoshkas, pink cones, golden fish and a red star on the top.

I guess she hates it because she is Jewish.

She manages to hide her Jewishness quite well, but her humour gives it away, especially after a few drops of cognac.

GRANNY. Ptui!

DASHA (*to* GRANNY). Gran, when you have an allergy, you don't spit, you sneeze!

GRANNY. Alright. Tell your mother I left the *borscht* on the stove. I'll come back in the morning. Enjoy tonight, sweetheart.

DASHA (*to us*). She leaves and I put on *Rock on Bones*.

The music starts playing.

It's the first time that I've prepared an extra gift for someone other than Mum and Gran.

It's Bakunin's *Statism and Anarchy* wrapped for Joe.

Tonight he will come to celebrate not only the New Year, but also the collapse of the Berlin Wall.

I remember when Mum found out about him.

MOTHER. You were raised for better things than lost thugs.

DASHA (*to* MOTHER). Don't you know his mother is a respected member of the Communist Party?

MOTHER. Really? Well, then it's time for me to meet him.

The clock chimes eleven.

DASHA (*to us*). It's time. But I'm still in my lousy T-shirt.

I see that Mum's long, perfectly ironed dress hangs from the door of her closet.

She made it from the sketches in the German magazine that I got from Alex's.

I open the cupboard and find a black, crumpled, overstretched skirt covered in dirt and petrol.

(*To* MOTHER.) Mum, I've got nothing to wear.

MOTHER. Choose anything you like from mine.

DASHA (*to us*). I see the most innocent blue dress with little white flowers.

(*To* MOTHER.) The blue one.

MOTHER. I was wearing it on the day you were born.

DASHA (*to us*). I squeeze my bum and try to wiggle into it.

It's tight but makes me look slim.

Pause.

I get out on the balcony.

It's dark. I lean on my toes and blow on the frozen glass.

In front of me frost patterns, street lights, snowflakes all combine in this winter dance.

As I turn back to the door, I see my reflection and behind it, my mum.

I look like her now.

I look like Mum.

Dark eyes, thin eyebrows and round breasts.

She smiles at me.

The doorbell rings.

It's Joe.

He stands here with a fishnet bag filled with oranges and a bottle of Soviet champagne.

First, he shakes the snow off his boots and then steps in.

I lead him into the kitchen with the pride of a little girl who is about to show her family her first sandcastle.

(*To* MOTHER.) Mum, this is Zhenya, he brought oranges. You can call him Joe.

MOTHER. Please sit down. You want some salad, James?

JOE. It's Joe. Yes, please.

MOTHER. So tell me, who are these anarchists?

JOE. As Kant once said: 'Anarchy is law and freedom without force.'

MOTHER. You can tell these lullabies to girls in short skirts but to me you're going to speak straight.

DASHA. Mum!

JOE. Basically, people think we need a government but, in fact, we can live without it… evolution occurs in groups, not individuals… even Greeks had what we call… a public administration.

MOTHER (*to* DASHA). He speaks like Lenin. I've got a bad feeling.

DASHA. Don't worry, Mum, we can take him down any time.

(*To* JOE.) Joe, can you fill Mum's glass?

The sound of chimes.

(*To us.*) We raise our glasses.

MOTHER. Happy nineteen ninety!

DASHA. On the table: Granny's *borscht*, grilled meat, beetroots and potatoes.

In the centre, little pieces of paper on which we'll write our wishes, burn them and drink the ashes.

Mum writes.

MOTHER. To see the ocean.

DASHA. I write 'to burn Gorbachev', melt it and down it.

Joe writes.

JOE. To take his place.

The sound of chimes stops. It's December 1990.

DASHA. A year later we're standing on the Red Square, forged together in a chain of bodies.

It's minus-thirty degrees.

Joe's addressing the people who are getting out of the department store GUM.

His voice is raspy, his legs are shaking.

JOE. Anarchy means different things, but tonight it's about helping Armenia. The government should know they failed their people. We want to support the victims of the earthquake. Whatever you donate to warm us up will be sent to Yerevan.

DASHA. I look around but I see only one glove from a boy who accidentally dropped it when he'd thrown a snowball at us.

No one wants to help.

JOE. Anarchists, stand still! Don't you dare run!

DASHA. I see a dark wave looming towards us.

(*To* JOE.) A storm? A flock?

JOE. No, it's the Kremlin Regiment!

DASHA (*to us*). Katya and the others run but we stand still.

I'm holding Joe's hand.

Dozens of men, six feet tall, red-and-blue uniforms.

They throw buckets of water at us.

My whole body turns into a giant piece of ice, so heavy that I can barely hold it upright.

I see Joe bending over from the cold.

(*To* JOE.) Joe, resist.

JOE. Where is everyone? Where are the anarchists?

DASHA. It's just us two.

JOE. They left?

DASHA. Don't give in.

JOE. It burns...

DASHA (*to us*). He falls.

Unconscious.

OFFICER. Is he your captain?

DASHA (*to* OFFICER). No.

OFFICER. Step aside.

DASHA. He's a *komsomol*. His mother's a member of the party. You need me. I'm an anarchist.

OFFICER. What's your name?

DASHA. Dasha. I just turned sixteen.

OFFICER. Dasha, you are arrested for hooliganism and anti-Soviet propaganda. You'll spend the next four weeks in jail and will never be allowed to attend university or college.

It's 1979.

DASHA (*to us*). I'm six and I only want one thing, to become Maria Callas.

I'm standing in the kitchen in my little green dress and tights looking up at Dad.

The room is warm and filled with light.

I want him to notice me but Mum is screaming.

MOTHER. I can't stand it any more!

DASHA. She gets a pair of keys from Dad's coat. They don't fit our door.

Dad is silent.

He's bent over a bowl of soup, scooping out the bottom.

I get underneath the table and try to climb on top of my dad.

Mum shouts at him.

MOTHER. Get out!

DASHA. I'm scared. I grab him by his arm.

> The bowl of soup spills all over him.

DAD. Get in here.

DASHA. I resist.

> He pulls me up from underneath the table.

DAD. Stand in the corner.

DASHA (*to* DAD). No!

> (*To us.*) I slap him on the chest.

> He lifts me up with his left arm and with the right continues arguing with Mum.

> He drags me through the kitchen door into the corridor and puts me down.

DAD. Stand still and face the wall.

DASHA. I turn.

> An inch from my nose I see a giant black hole.

> Eight eyes. Eight legs. Hairy.

> (*To* DAD.) Spider!

DAD. Stop it.

DASHA (*to us*). He presses me from behind.

> I stand here alone. Facing it.

> An inch away.

> Stares at me.

> One-on-one. Fair.

> He bites. I die.

> Because my dad doesn't believe me.

> *The sound of chimes.*

JOE. Happy New Year.

DASHA. They allowed me one call.

JOE. How is it over there?

DASHA (*to* JOE). They shaved my head.

JOE. It's okay. Just try to keep your teeth. Hair grows fast.

DASHA. How did it end?

JOE. We didn't send a damn thing to Armenia...

DASHA. It was very cold, Joe.

JOE. I know. Katya lost her right arm, so I guess she'll have to play the piano with one hand.

DASHA. Don't be so tough on them.

JOE. Don't you understand? If they didn't run, you wouldn't be there. They betrayed us!

DASHA. Joe, they ran for their lives. The anarchists are all we've got. You must trust them.

OFFICER. Time's up!

DASHA. I have to go... say to Mum and Gran... that I'm alright.

The State Anthem of the Soviet Union is playing.

(*To us.*) On December twenty-fifth, nineteen ninety-one, Mikhail Gorbachev will appear on television.

He'll resign from his post as president of the Soviet Union, the red flag will be lowered, and the State Anthem will be played for the last time.

But we're nine months away from that and the anarchists are planning the largest coup in Soviet history.

It's March 1991.

It's the eighth of March. The day when I officially move in with Joe.

It's late in the evening and he's writing a manifesto.

I stand behind him.

The anthem stops playing.

(*To* JOE.) Why do you leave your stuff on the floor? Such a cliché.

JOE. They say Yeltsin is a drunk.

DASHA. Then let's add poison to Granny's *samogon* and send it to him.

JOE. Is she still making it?

DASHA. You bet. I've got it in my bag.

JOE takes the bottle, drinks from it then hands it to her.

JOE. Come on!

DASHA. No, thanks.

JOE. Take it.

DASHA. I don't want it.

JOE. Have some.

DASHA. I'm pregnant.

JOE. What?

Pause. JOE shouts in excitement.

DASHA. Don't shout.

JOE. I can't... I'll be a dad!

DASHA. I doubt it.

JOE. Is it a boy? A girl's even better. I love girls... wait, what did you say?

DASHA. I'm not sure I want a kid.

JOE. Why not?

DASHA. Look outside! People queue for twelve hours for a plate of rice and half a sausage. The Mafia owns all the factories and shops. My mother lost her job.

JOE. Once we take over, we'll fix this.

DASHA. What if the coup goes wrong?

JOE. It won't.

DASHA. What if the anarchists fail?

JOE. I won't allow it, you understand! It's part of life. It's part of growing up. I know you are scared but I'll be there for you. You're growing a new pair of hands. A little anarchist...

You're my family, the only person I love and trust. Dasha, look at me.

She looks at him.

This is our legacy, our dream, this child is going to be the next leader of this country.

Pause.

DASHA (*to us*). I love Joe.

But the more time goes by the more I feel sick and weak.

I cannot work, walk or think.

My body gets in the way of who I am and what I believe.

I fall asleep during the discussions and miss protests because of constant nausea.

I feel poisoned.

I feel poisoned by Joe.

My pregnancy is an obstacle and seeing him capable, strong, fearless kills me.

I realise that he'll never understand because he'll never have to go through this.

So I call Mum and ask her to come with me.

Pause.

Early morning, a hospital corridor, Mum is on my left.

She brought a pair of woollen socks and a Thermos with strong black tea.

(*To* MOTHER.) This tea is perfect. Only you can make it like this.

MOTHER. Careful, it's hot.

DASHA. Will it hurt?

MOTHER. A bit... but you think of something nice.

DASHA (*to us*). In the nineties having an abortion is not a big deal.

In front of me there are nine women, from early teens to past forty.

They do it 'raw' here, without anaesthetics.

Mum pours Granny's *samogon* into the cup of tea. I down it.

Pause.

It's my turn.

I give her the cup, her hand is ice cold.

She is as white as the wall but looks at me with so much love and hope.

(*To* MOTHER.) Mum, revolution or hopelessness?

Pause.

MOTHER. Go with God.

DASHA (*to us*). I go into the room. Shut the door. The first thing I see is a bin filled with bloody tissues.

The doc is an old man with a grey beard. He looks like a Santa Claus.

GYNAECOLOGIST. How old are you?

DASHA (*to* GYNAECOLOGIST). Seventeen.

GYNAECOLOGIST. When did you become sexually active?

DASHA. Thirteen.

GYNAECOLOGIST. Do you smoke?

DASHA. Yes.

GYNAECOLOGIST. How many a day?

DASHA. A pack.

GYNAECOLOGIST. To abort the fetus it must be three months old.

DASHA. Mine is old enough.

Pause.

(*To us*.) I'm on the table.

Someone grabs my hand.

(*To* NURSE.) Mum?

(*To us*.) A mask. A nurse.

NURSE. Will be painful now.

DASHA. She has kind eyes just like Mum's.

The doctor comes over.

I turn.

He is an inch from me.

Spreads my legs.

Stares.

One-on-one. Fair.

NURSE. Hold on to me.

DASHA. He inserts a suction tube.

It burns.

I close my eyes.

Big breath.

Pause.

Gone.

Pause.

I'm home.

Joe comes in.

JOE *leaves. The sound of the door shutting.* DASHA *falls asleep.*

KATYA. Everyone is in the room. You have to start the coup!

DASHA (*to* KATYA). Where's Joe?

KATYA. I saw him outside. He'll come up.

DASHA You think something bad happened to him?

KATYA. Dasha, go for it.

DASHA (*to us*). I take the stand.

I look at their faces lit up by hope and light.

Joe will be proud of us.

(*To the anarchists*.) Tonight we're going to take over the government and prevent the Declaration of Belarusian Independence.

Sound of the doorbell ringing.

If the old Soviets hand the power to their own man, it'll be a continuation of autocracy.

Sound of the doorbell ringing.

You might ask 'Why am I here listening to this woman? What is this anarchy after all?' Well, it can be different things... but it's never chaos. What does anarchy mean to you? To me it means...

The sound of a gunshot.

OFFICER. Everybody down!

Bang. DASHA *gets on the ground.*

DASHA (*to us*). Gas.

I can't breathe.

I can't believe my eyes. It's Joe, leading the police into our base.

Twenty men with rifles.

(*To* JOE.) Joe, what's going on?

(*To us*.) He points at me.

JOE. It's her.

DASHA. Joe?

JOE. Face the wall!

DASHA (*to us*). I turn.

Two men press me from behind.

JOE. You took away my dream.

Pause.

DASHA. I see a giant black hole.

Eight eyes. Eight legs. Hairy.

I grab it.

I can see its legs coming out between my little fingers.

Bang.

The end of the flashbacks.

BOSS. I'm seriously impressed. Here's a fat envelope with your pay plus my personal gratitude for your comradeship.

DASHA (*to* BOSS). Thanks, boss. By the way, Sanych turned up drunk, harassed a worker.

BOSS. I thought he only drinks milk. Well... it's going to be bloody tonight, so stay safe.

DASHA (*to us*). I push the door.

Go.

Down the stairs.

Through the hall.

Pass the gates.

Street.

Crowds of people carrying new flags, white-and-red.

They are building barricades from rubbish bins, shopping carts and plastic crates.

At the bus stop I'm waiting for the sixty-eight that will take me to Terminal One.

I'm an hour away from the departure gate.

I sit on a bench. One last smoke.

Before every protest Katya and I used to share a cigarette.

Will I be able to afford them abroad?

Pause.

Well... I've never been abroad.

Someone screams: 'Help!'

I turn and see that behind me a riot policeman is beating up a kid with a baton.

The boy is on the ground holding on to the white-and-red flag.

I stand up, grab the bag and sprint.

(*To* POLICEMAN.) You pig!

(*To us*.) I hit him with the bag.

My bras, pants, cables fly out.

I pick them up and throw them at his leg, his face, his arm.

The pig stops.

The kid runs off.

Pause.

It's just us two.

I'm trembling. Leg is bleeding.

I feel like Luke Skywalker about to fight Darth Vader.

Only my force has long gone.

Pause.

As I step back he runs at me.

We crash on the ground.

He jumps up and kicks me in the guts.

I'm folded in half.

He kneels, clenches his fists and hits hard.

The punches are so strong that I can hear the cracking of my bones.

I crawl forward.

He grabs my hair and pulls me backwards.

I cling to his arm.

He turns my head and spits in my face, then smears it all over.

I spit at him too, with blood.

I try to stay upright but I collapse.

I roll my head closer to my chest.

I hold my breath.

His baton jumps off my ribs like a squash ball.

The pain hasn't come yet. Only the taste of metal.

The only thing that's left is to stay still, to play dead.

Across the road someone screams: 'Police!'

He stops.

Pause.

He places his foot on my hip and shakes it to see if he's killed.

Unzips.

Pulls out.

A hot stream of urine pours down my skin.

I quietly inhale the smell of ammonia, dampness, and pavement dust.

POLICEMAN. Get up, you cunt.

DASHA. I keep still with my head to the ground listening to every sound.

He's gone.

The sound of a minibus horn.

DRIVER. You alright?

DASHA (*to* DRIVER). I'm fine.

DRIVER. I'm heading to Minsk National Airport. You need a ride?

DASHA. Are there any showers at the airport?

DRIVER. Not that I know of. Why?

DASHA. Well… when is the next one?

DRIVER. Half-hour.

DASHA. I'll be back.

(*To us.*) He slides the door and goes.

I watch him vanish through the blur of traffic lights.

It hurts but I get up. Confident. Been there.

I take off my torn tights, adjust the dress, then tie my hair up.

I collect my things one by one, leaving out only the Pringles can.

I hold it.

I hold you.

Mama.

Pause.

At the bottom I see her ashes.

She died almost thirty years ago from a sedative overdose.

On the twenty-fifth of August nineteen ninety-one.

On the day when the police broke into the flat and took us all in.

The day when Lukashenko's predecessor declared Belarus independent.

The day Joe turned us in, two policemen did a prank on my mum.

The sound of the doorbell ringing.

MOTHER. Who's there?

OFFICER. Are you Dasha's mum?

MOTHER. Yes.

OFFICER. We regret to inform you but your daughter blew herself up with a bottle bomb.

DASHA. That night she put on that innocent blue dress with flowers and sat on the chair, in our kitchen, leaning against the fridge.

All night she was drinking her drops with Granny's *samogon.*

By the time I got home she was gone.

She was the only person I was fighting for... the reason I joined the anarchists.

I'll never forgive Joe for this.

Pause.

Since then I keep her in this Pringles can.

Salt and vinegar.

She hated vinegar.

Pause.

I wonder if there are any yellow bits at the bottom.

Can she feel them?

I wrapped her in this dark-blue paper.

Ocean colour.

All she ever wanted was to see the ocean.

The sound of men marching on the street. On the radio there is an announcement that Lukashenko has won with eighty per cent of the votes.

I see dozens of our workers marching towards the centre.

From the Lego toys they've turned into one whole regiment.

Each one of them is a soldier.

Pause.

I'm one of them.

I'm one of these men.

I've turned into a humble pacifist but my hand is still as heavy as a hammer.

For centuries they've been holding a lid over our heads.

We have no voice, no means, no rights – we are a grey mess not a mass.

We're on the menu for those foreign papers, handshakes, speeches, sanctions, negotiations.

But here I am... a middle-aged freak, outworn Themis.

So what does anarchy mean to me?

It means justice.

Pause.

I go to the nearest kiosk where I buy acetone and a large bottle of vodka.

I have a few sips and the rest I pour down on my bleeding hands and knees.

On the road I stop a motorcyclist who pumps some gas off his tank.

I compress the Green Card into the mixture.

I tear the bottom of my mum's dress and stick it into the bottleneck.

Pause.

I get to the centre.

I'm on top of the bridge above the River Svislach.

I gently unwrap the Pringles can. Her favourite colour. Dark blue.

Time to say goodbye.

Pause.

Thirty years of silence.

It's time for you to see the ocean.

I'll stay here… the waters will take you.

She spreads the ashes all around her as if drawing a rainbow.

Go, see the world.

Go with God.

Mama.

Pause.

The ashes scatter against the sunset like glitter and disappear into the river.

I hold the empty Pringles can and the Molotov cocktail.

As a crowd of protesters reaches the bridge, I dive into them as into a swarm of bees.

Like a tide we arrive in front of the City Hall.

Through all the people I push the rest of my limbs and remains forward.

Some push me away, others push me further from behind.

I find myself in the place where I first came to the protest with the anarchists.

The same spot where once it was twenty of us, now there are thousands.

I remember sitting on top of Joe's shoulders and looking at the open window.

'There is a reason why you are here, don't look back.'

The sound of sirens.

On a concrete stage I see men in suits and riot police.

I see Joe's back facing me. I know it's him.

Broad shoulders, tilted head and a beam of dark curls that look like a kippah on his bald head.

He's a corrupt right-wing member of the House of Representatives.

Many times I've thought, when the day comes and I see him, what will I say?

I throw the empty Pringles can at his feet.

He turns, picks it up and looks at the crowd.

I smile.

Pause.

He sees me.

This time I won't miss.

She lights up the wick.

It's time.

She tosses the Molotov cocktail.

Blackout.

A Nick Hern Book

The Anarchist first published in Great Britain in 2022 as a paperback original by Nick Hern Books Limited, The Glasshouse, 49a Goldhawk Road, London W12 8QP, in association with Woven Voices and Jermyn Street Theatre, London

The Anarchist copyright © 2022 Karina Wiedman

Karina Wiedman has asserted her right to be identified as the author of this work

Cover artwork by Ciaran Walsh

Designed and typeset by Nick Hern Books, London
Printed in Great Britain by Mimeo Ltd, Huntingdon, Cambridgeshire PE29 6XX

A CIP catalogue record for this book is available from the British Library

ISBN   978 1 83904 113 6

Woodland CARBON
www.woodlandcarbon.co.uk
NICK HERN BOOKS
Printed on Carbon Captured paper